P9-CWE-388

Do It!
Play Recorder

A World of Musical Enjoyment At Your Fingertips

Student Book One

James O. Froseth

Contributing Editors: Marguerite Wilder & Carolee Stewart

Available in the following configurations:
Student book only (MLR-437)
Student book plus compact disc (MLR-438)
Student book plus compact disc plus recorder (MLR-440)
Compact disc only (MLR-436)
Teacher's Edition (MLR-441)

Copyright © 1996 GIA Publications, Inc.
7404 S. Mason Ave., Chicago, IL 60638

THE RECORDER EMBOUCHURE

The word embouchure (pronounced ah´m-bu-shure) refers to the position and use of the lips and facial muscles in producing a musical tone on a wind instrument. Tone quality, intonation, and articulation depend heavily on development of correct embouchure and breath control.

Check your embouchure regularly by practicing in front of a mirror.

A. Positon the lips on the mouth-piece as if pronouncing the syllable DU (Dew) (The teeth should not touch the mouth-piece).

B. Seal the lips with a gentle inward pucker.

SKILLS CHECK-OFF

Step	Week			
	1	2	3	4
A				
B				

INSTRUMENT POSITION AND HAND POSITION

In order to develop technical skill on the recorder you must first establish correct posture, correct instrument position, and correct hand position. Correct hand position begins with proper posture. Correct hand position requires curved fingers. When fingers are straight, finger joints are locked and tense. When fingers are curved, finger joints are unlocked and relaxed. Always keep your fingers curved when playing to avoid muscular tension. Use a mirror regularly to check your instrument position and hand position.

A. Position the left hand to the top of the recorder.

B. Curve the fingers.

C. Keep the thumb straight.

D. Keep the wrist straight.

E. Position the right hand to the bottom of the recorder.

F. Place the fleshy pad of the thumb on the instrument approximately below and between the 4th and 5th holes.

G. Curve the fingers.

H. Keep the thumb straight.

I. Keep the wrist straight.

J. Position elbows comfortably away from the body.

CHECK

Step	Week			
	1	2	3	4
A				
B				
C				
D				
E				
F				
G				
H				
I				
J				

BREATHING AND BREATH CONTROL

Proper breathing and breath control are important elements of recorder playing. Tone quality, intonation, musical phrasing, and expression all require control of the breath.

It takes a very light and very steady stream of air to produce a musical tone on the recorder. If the air stream is too heavy or too fast the tone will sound shrill and out-of-tune. A slow or unsteady stream of air will cause the tone to sound weak and out-of-tune.

IMAGINARY BREATH CONTROL EXPERIMENT

A. Imagine a lighted candle below and 4 to 6 inches away from your mouth.

B. Now, bend the flame over with a light and steady stream of air.

C. Sustain the breath to hold the flame in a bent-over position for 5 to 10 seconds.

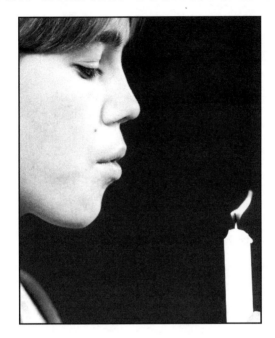

SKILLS CHECK-OFF				
	Week			

Step	1	2	3	4
A				
B				

C				

ARTICULATION

Articulation refers to how the tone is started and how it is stopped. This important aspect of instrumental performance requires correct posture, correct breathing and breath control, and a good embouchure.

STARTING THE TONE

A tone is started when a stream of air from the lungs sets an air column vibrating inside the recorder. The tongue acts as a valve that releases the air stream. Figure 1 shows the position of the tongue on the roof of the mouth behind the front teeth prior to the start of the tone. Figure 2 illustrates the position of the tongue after the tone has begun. NOTE: The lower jaw remains stable while tonguing.

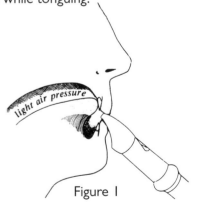

Figure 1

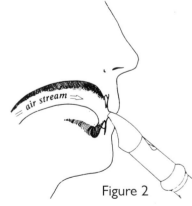

Figure 2

There are two acceptable ways to stop a tone. The first is by stopping the air stream. This method is used at the end of a long tone, before a silence in the music, and for separated styles bref articulation. Pronounce the syllables "tu", "tu", "tu", "tu", with a space after each syllable to simulate a separated style of articulation. The second way to stop the tone is by simply touching the roof of the mouth behind the front teeth quickly and lightly with the tongue. This method is used for fast tonguing and for a connected style of articulation. To simulate a connected style of articulation pronounce the syllables "du—du—du—du—" with the sensation that the air flow is continous. Avoid articulation that sounds like the syllables "thoot", "hu", "thut", or "hoot".

"YOU CAN LOOK IT UP"
MUSIC SIGNS AND SYMBOLS DICTIONARY
VOCABULARY NEEDED TO NAME, IDENTIFY, AND DESCRIBE

SIGN/SYMBOL and NAME	DESCRIPTION/INTERPRETATION

Staff — The **Staff** is composed of five lines and four spaces.

Ledger Line — The **Ledger Line** is a short line used to extend the staff.

Bar Line / Double Bar Line — The **Bar Line** is a vertical line used to divide a staff into measures.

The **Double Bar Line** is two lines used to indicate the end of the music or the end of a section of music.

The space between two bar lines is called a **Measure**

Repeat Sign — **Repeat Sign**: "Repeat from the beginning or repeat a section between two repeat signs."

First and Second Ending — **First and Second Ending:** "Play from the beginning and to the repeat sign in the first ending. Then, return to the beginning. On the repeat, skip the first ending and continue through the second ending.

Treble Clef (G Clef) — The **Treble Clef** is a sign used to fix the pitch of the second line of the staff to G.

LINES   SPACES

E G B D F   F A C E

Letter Names are letters of the alphabet used to name and to identify the lines and spaces of the Treble Clef.

♯ **Sharp** — A **Sharp** is a sign used to raise the pitch of a note one half-step (one semi-tone).

♭ **Flat** — A **Flat** is a sign to lower the pitch of a note one half-step (one semi-tone).

♮ **Natural** — A **Natural** is a sign used to cancel a sharp or flat in a measure or in the key signature.

Key Signatures

C Major G Major D Major F Major
A Minor E Minor B Minor D Minor

A **Key Signature** is the particular arrangement of flats or sharps that appears at the beginning of each staff to indicate the key of a piece or composition.

Accent — An **Accent** is a symbol to indicate special stress or emphasis on a certain note.

Staccato — A **Staccato** sign is used to indicate a shortened or separated style of articulation.

Tenuto — A **Tenuto** sign over or below a note is used to indicate a sustained (connected) style of articulation.

Tie — The **Tie** is a curved line used to connect two notes of the same pitch. The first note is tongued; the second is not.

Slur   The **Slur** is a curved line above or below two or more notes of different pitch to indicate a connected style of performance. That is, on one breath line without tongued articulation.

,   **Breath Mark**   The **Breath Mark** is a sign used to indicate the appropriate place to take a breath.

NOTES	RESTS	
o	—	**Whole (United Kingdom - Semi Breve)**
♩	—	**Half (UK - Minim)**
♩.	—.	**Dotted Half (UK - Dotted Minim)**
♩	₹	**Quarter (UK - Crotchet)**
♩.	₹ ⁊	**Dotted Quarter (UK - Dotted Crotchet)**
♪	⁊	**Eighth (UK - Quaver)**
♫		**Barred Eighths (UK - Barred Quavers)**
♬	⁊	**Sixteenth (UK - Semi Quaver)**
♬		**Barred Sixteenths (UK - Barred Semi Quavers)**

INTERPRETATION

The Rhythmic Values of Notes and Rests Are Determined By the Measure Signature. (See Measure Signatures below.)

MEASURE (TIME) SIGNATURES

Two-Quarter Measure Signature   Two Beats In Each Measure
The Quarter Note Is The Primary Beat (Crotchet)

Two-Half (Cut-Time) Measure Signature   Two Beats In Each Measure
The Half Note Is The Primary Beat (Minim)

Four-Quarter (Common) Measure Signature   Four Beats In Each Measure
The Quarter Note Is The Primary Beat (Crotchet)

Three-Quarter Measure Signature

1. One Beat In Each Measure
   The Dotted Half Note Is The Primary Beat (Dotted Minim)

2. Three Beats In Each Measure
   The Quarter Note Is The Primary Beat (Crotchet)

Six-Eighth Measure Signature

1. Two Beats In Each Measure
   The Dotted Quarter Note Is The Primary Beat (Dotted Crotchet)

2. Six Beats In Each Measure
   The Eighth Note Is The Primary Beat (Quaver)

6

FIRST TONES

FOLK SONG — *A song reflecting the traditions of the people of a country or region and forming part of their characteristic culture.*

SOLO — *One player, alone, with or without accompaniment.*

CD
SOLO #1
ACCOM. #2

1 **Hot Cross Buns**

Moderato*

English Folk Song

Hot cross buns, Hot cross buns, One cent, Two cents, Hot cross buns.

HONKY TONK — *A Rowdy musical style characterized by a lively piano accompaniment.*

CD
SOLO #3
ACCOM. #4

2 ★ SOLO **Hot Cross Buns** (HONKY TONK STYLE STARTING ON B)

ROCK AND ROLL — *A mid-1950s style of popular music featuring guitar and driving rhythms with accents on the off-beats:* | **2** | **2**

CD
SOLO #5
ACCOM. #6

3 ★★ SOLO **Hot Cross Buns** (ROCK AND ROLL STYLE - "BY EAR" STARTING ON B)

CD
SOLO #7
ACCOM. #8

4 **Notes**

Moderato

U.S.

Notes step down, Notes step up. Notes re - peat and notes can skip.

BLUE GRASS — *A type of Anglo-American folk music originating around the mid-1940s in rural Appalachia.*

CD
SOLO #9
ACCOM. #9-2

5 **Mary Had A Little Lamb**

Lively

(,)

Traditional Folk Song

Mar-y had a lit-tle lamb. Lit-tle lamb. Lit-tle lamb. Mar-y had a lit-tle lamb with fleece as white as snow.

REGGAE — *A musical style mixing African and Caribbean rhythms often attributed to Jamaican sources.*

CD
SOLO #10
ACCOM. #10-2

6 ★ SOLO **Mary Had A Little Lamb** (REGGAE STYLE STARTING ON B)

CD
SOLO #11
ACCOM. #11-2

7 ★★ SOLO **Mary Had A Little Lamb** (ROCK AND ROLL STYLE "BY EAR" ON B - WITH REPEAT)

? *Forget the meaning of something?* **You Can Look It Up** in the **Music Terms Dictionary** on pages 42, 43, 44, and 45.

SOLO #12
ACCOM. #12-2

1 **Au Claire de la Lune**

Legato

French Folk Song

Au clair de la lu - ne, Mon a - mi Pier - rot,
In the moon's pale shim - mer, My dear friend, Pier - rot,

Prê - te - moi ta plu - me, Pour é - crite un mot.
I would like to write you, Just a word or so.

SOLO #13
ACCOM. #13-2

2 **Down By The Station**

Moderato

American School Song

Down by the sta - tion ear - ly in the morn - ing,

Down by the sta - tion hear the whis - tle blow.

JAZZ — *Originally a style of improvised dance music characterized by strong rhythms and expressiveness, originating in the South by Black Americans.*

SOLO #14
ACCOM. #15

3 ★ **SOLO Down by the Station** (JAZZ STYLE "BY EAR" STARTING ON G - WITH REPEAT)

LULLABY — *A cradle, song usually sung by a mother to soothe or quiet an infant before bedtime.*

SOLO #16
ACCOM. #16-2

4 **Fais do do**

Legato

French Lullaby

Fais do - do, Co - las, mon p'tit fre - re, Fais do - do, T'au - ras, du lo - lo.
Go to sleep my sweet lit - tle bro - ther, Go to sleep, and you'll get a treat.

THEME AND VARIATIONS — *A musical form based upon a melody followed by a succession of composed rhythmic/melodic variations.*

SOLO #17
ACCOM. #18

5 **Stepping and Skipping** (THEME)

Moderato

U.S.

Step - ping, step - ping, step - ping up. Skip - ping, skip - ping, step and skip.

ACCOM. #18

6 **Variation One**

ACCOM. #18

7 **Variation Two**

? *Forget the name of something?* **You Can Look It Up** *in the* **Music Signs and Symbols Dictionary** *on Pages 2 and 3.*

8

SOLO #5
ACCOM. #6

1 Hot Cross Buns

Moderato

English Folk Song

Hot cross buns. Hot cross buns. One a pen-ny, Two a pen-ny, Hot cross buns.

DUET — *A composition for two performers.*

ACCOM. #2

Taking Turns Duet

Moderato

English Folk Song

2

Hot cross buns, One a pen-ny. Hot. Buns.

3

Hot cross buns, Two a pen-ny. Cross.

SOLO #19
ACCOM. #19-2

4 Rocket Cruiser

Moderato

U.S.

Wish I had a rock-et crui-ser and a base on Mars. I could fly a-way to dis-tant stars.

ACCOM. #8

5 More Notes

Moderato

U.S.

Notes step down, Notes can step on up. Notes can sub-di-vide and notes can skip.

ACCOM. #8

Eighth Notes Duet

Moderato

U.S.

6

7

? *Forget the meaning of something?* **You Can Look It Up** *in the* **Music Terms Dictionary** *on pages 42, 43, 44, and 45.*

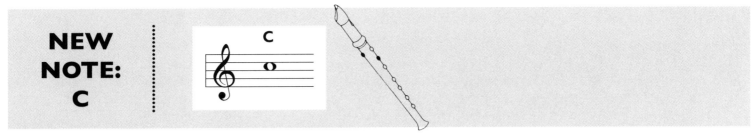

NEW NOTE: C

REGGAE — A musical style mixing African and Caribbean rhythms often attributed to Jamaican sources.

SOLO #20
ACCOM. #21

1 **Cobbler, Cobbler**

Rhythmically

Jamaican Street Song

Cob - bler, Cob - bler fix my shoe, Get it done by half past two.

Half past two, I'm at your door, Get it done by half past four.

ACCOM. #21

2 **Variation on Cobbler, Cobbler**

Fix my shoe, Half past two. At the door, Wait no more.

IMPROVISATION — *The art of creating music spontaneously, during performance. Also, a form of composition.*

RHYTHMIC IMPROVISATION — *The act of expressing one's own rhythmic ideas while maintaining the basic melodic character of the piece.*

ACCOM. #21

3 ★ SOLO **Improvise rhythmic variations on Cobbler, Cobbler**

BLUE GRASS — A type of Anglo-American folk music originating around the mid-1940s in rural Appalachia.

SOLO #22
ACCOM. #23

4 **Juba**

Playfully

African-American Folk Song

Ju - ba this and Ju - ba that. Ju - ba chased a yel - low cat,

Ju - ba up and Ju - ba down, Ju - ba run - ning all a - round.

ACCOM. #23

5 **Variation on Juba**

ACCOM. #23

6 ★ SOLO **Improvise rhythmic variations on Juba**

? ♫ *Forget the sound of a rhythm pattern?* **You Can Look It Up** *in the* **Rhythm Pattern Dictionary** *on pages 46 and 47.*

BARCAROLLE — *Originally, a folk song of the Venetian gondoliers (boatmen of the Italian city of Venice).*

SOLO #24
ACCOM. #24-2

I **Barcarolle**

Smoothly - In one

Jacques Offenbach (1819-1880)

POLKA — *A lively dance originated by Bohemian (Eastern European) peasants.*

SOLO #25
ACCOM. #25-2

2 **Polka**

Cheerfully

Dance Tune

ACCOM. #25-2

3 **Variations on Polka**

SPIRITUAL — *A religious folk song of African-American origin.*

SOLO #26
ACCOM. #26-2

4 **Jacob Drink**

With enthusiasm

U. S. Spiritual

ACCOM. #26-2

5 **Variation on Jacob Drink**

6 **Shave and a Haircut**

As quickly as possible

Early American

Shave   and   a   hair - cut,   TWO   BITS!

? *Forget the fingering of a note?* **You Can Look It Up** *on the* **Fingering Chart** *located on the inside front cover.*

THEME AND VARIATIONS — *A musical form based upon a melody followed by a succession of composed rhythmic/melodic variations.*

WALTZ — *A 19th century dance in triple meter.*

SOLO #27
ACCOM. #27-2

1 Waltz Theme with Variations

Lightly   Dance Tune

ACCOM. #27-2

2 Waltz Variation One

ACCOM. #27-2

3 Waltz Variation Two

ACCOM. #27-2

4 Waltz Variation Three

SOLO #28
ACCOM. #28-2

5 Gólya, Gólya, Gilice (The Storks)

Plaintively   Hungarian Folk Song

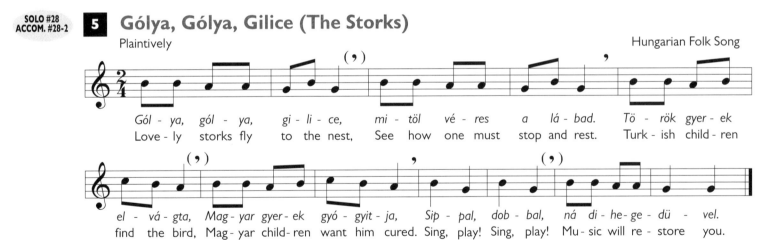

Gól - ya, gól - ya, gi - li - ce, mi - töl vé - res a lá - bad. Tö - rök gyer - ek
Love - ly storks fly to the nest, See how one must stop and rest. Turk - ish child - ren

el - vá - gta, Mag - yar gyer - ek gyó - gyit - ja, Sip - pal, dob - bal, ná di - he - ge - dü - vel.
find the bird, Mag - yar child - ren want him cured. Sing, play! Sing, play! Mu - sic will re - store you.

BRANLE — *A popular French group dance of the 16th century in which all the motions of the lead couple are imitated.*

SOLO #29
ACCOM. #29-2

6 Champaigne Branle

Lively   16th Century French Dance Tune
                                                                    Claude Gervaise

? *Forget the meaning of something?* **You Can Look It Up** *in the* **Music Terms Dictionary** *on pages 42, 43, 44, and 45.*

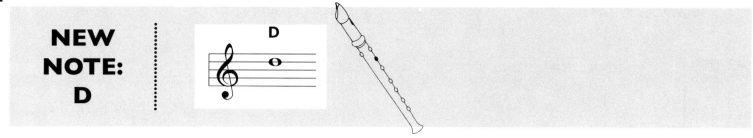

NEW NOTE: D

BLUES — *An African-American folk music characterized by spontaneity and deep emotion.*

SLUR — *A curved line* ⌒ *above or below two or more notes of different pitch to indicate a connected style of performance. That is, on one breath line without tongued articulation.*

SOLO #30
ACCOM. #32

1 **The Blues in D**
In a swinging style

CALL AND RESPONSE — *A musical alteration between two performers or a performer and a group of performers. The musical response to the call may be imitated or improvised.*

CALL AND
RESPONCE #31

2 ★ SOLO **The Blues in D** (IMITATIVE CALL AND RESPONSE - "BY EAR" STARTING ON D)

EXAMPLE: **Call**   **Response (Imitated)**

IMPROVISATION — *The art of creating music spontaneously, during performance. Also, a form of composition.*

CALL AND
RESPONCE #31

3 ★★ SOLO **The Blues in D** (IMPROVISED CALL AND RESPONSE - "BY EAR" ON ANY NOTE)

EXAMPLE: **Call**   **Response (Improvised)**

ACCOM. #32

4 ★★★ SOLO (IMPROVISE OVER THE 12 BAR BLUES IN D "BY EAR")

D   C   A   G   A   C   D

? *Forget the name of something?* **You Can Look It Up** *on pages 4 and 5.*

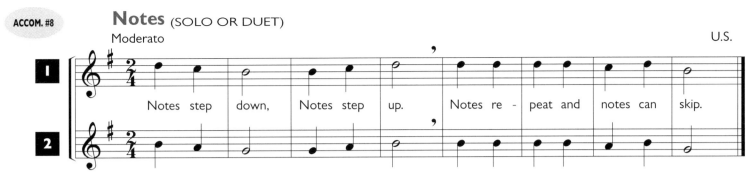

Notes (SOLO OR DUET)

ACCOM. #8

Moderato

U.S.

1

Notes step down, Notes step up. Notes re - peat and notes can skip.

2

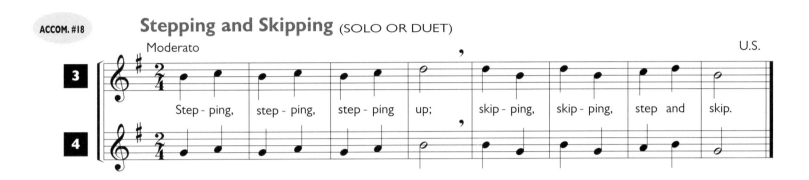

Stepping and Skipping (SOLO OR DUET)

ACCOM. #18

Moderato

U.S.

3

Step - ping, step - ping, step - ping up; skip - ping, skip - ping, step and skip.

4

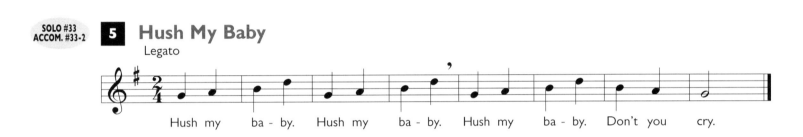

SOLO #33
ACCOM. #33-2

5 **Hush My Baby**

Legato

Hush my ba - by. Hush my ba - by. Hush my ba - by. Don't you cry.

ROUND — *A specially composed melody that allows two or more individuals to create interesting musical effects by starting the melody at different times.*

METRONOME MARKING — *A precise indication of the speed of the beat as expressed by Maelzel's metronome. (The metronome is a machine with a ticking pendulum patented by Johann Maelzel in 1816. M.M. ♩ = 96 means the tempo of the quarter note is 96 beats per minute.)*

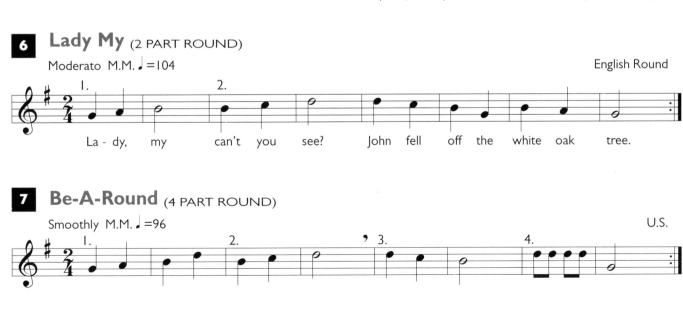

6 **Lady My** (2 PART ROUND)

Moderato M.M. ♩ =104

English Round

1. La - dy, my can't you 2. see? John fell off the white oak tree.

7 **Be-A-Round** (4 PART ROUND)

Smoothly M.M. ♩ =96

U.S.

1. 2. 3. 4.

Forget the sound of a rhythm pattern? **You Can Look It Up** *in the* **Rhythm Pattern Dictionary** *on pages 46 and 47.*

SOLO #34
ACCOM. #34-2

1 **Lightly Row**

Lively

Old German Folk Tune

Light - ly row, light - ly row, o'er the shin - ing waves we go;

Smooth - ly glide, smooth - ly glide, on the si - lent tide.

COUNTRY SWING — *A blend of western, bluegrass and swing styles originating in Texas during the 1940s.*

SOLO #35
ACCOM. #35-2

2 ★ SOLO **Lightly Row** (COUNTRY SWING STYLE - "BY EAR" STARTING ON D)

SOLO #36
ACCOM. #36-2

3 ★★ SOLO **Lightly Row** (QUICK TIME)

Old German Folk Tune

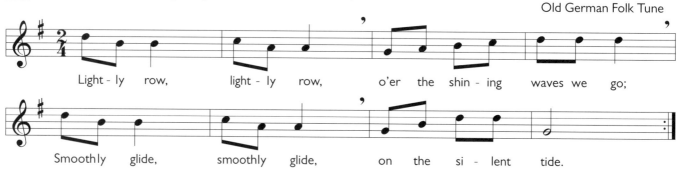

Light - ly row, light - ly row, o'er the shin - ing waves we go;

Smoothly glide, smoothly glide, on the si - lent tide.

SOLO #37
ACCOM. #37-2

4 **Norwegian Dance**

Lively

Scandinavian Folk Tune

5 **Round Dance** (4 PART ROUND)

Lightly M.M. ♩. = 100

U.S.

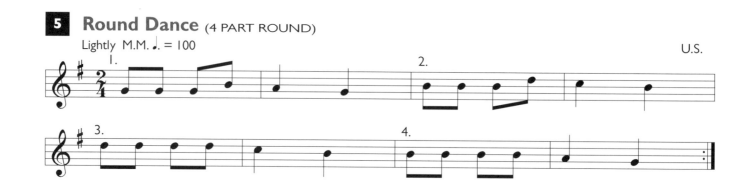

? *Forget the name of something?* **You Can Look It Up** *in the* **Music Signs and Symbols Dictionary** *on Pages 2 and 3.*

THEME AND VARIATIONS *

Forget the name of something? **You Can Look It Up** in the **Music Signs and Symbols Dictionary** on Pages 2 and 3.

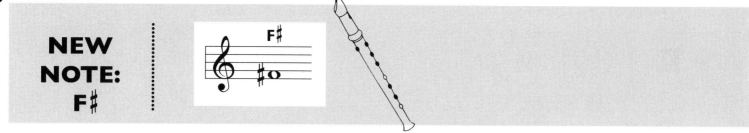

NEW NOTE: F♯

SOLO #45
ACCOM. #45-2

A Paris (SOLO OR DUET)

Moderato

Old French Tune

A Pa - ris, a Pa - ris, sur un pe - tit che - val gris.
To Pa - ree, to Pa - ree, on a hum - ble grey - haired steed.

HYMN — *A song of worship.*

SOLO #46
ACCOM. #46-2

Vesper Hymn (SOLO OR DUET)

Smooth and connected

Russian Folk Tune
Text by Thomas Moore

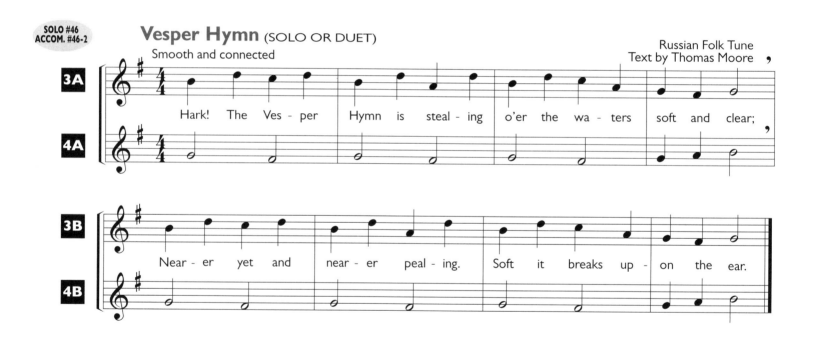

Hark! The Ves - per Hymn is steal - ing o'er the wa - ters soft and clear;

Near - er yet and near - er peal - ing. Soft it breaks up - on the ear.

5 **We Are Met** (4 PART ROUND)

Brightly M.M. ♩ = 120

Samuel Webbe (c. 1680)

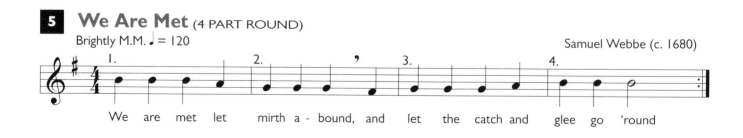

We are met let mirth a - bound, and let the catch and glee go 'round

LULLABY — *A cradle song usually sung by a mother to soothe or quiet an infant before bedtime.*

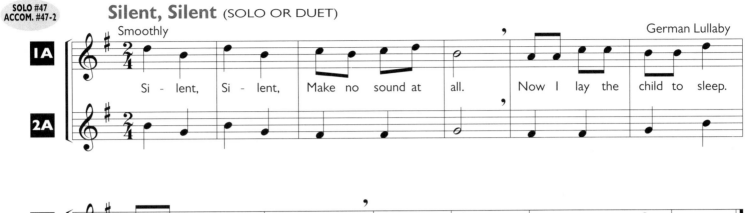

SLUR — *A curved line*  *above or below two or more notes of different pitch to indicate a connected style of performance. That is, on one breath line without tongued articulation.*

Bubble Gum Duet

SPECIAL PROJECT — **Learn to Play a Song "By Ear"**

5 ★★★ **SOLO Suggestion: Play *Go Tell Aunt Rhody* Starting on B**

NATURAL (♮) — *A sign that cancels a flat (♭) or sharp (♯) in the measure or in the key signature.*

6 French Cathedrals (3 PART ROUND)

? *Forget the fingering of a note?* **You Can Look It Up** on the **Fingering Chart** located on the inside front cover.

COUNTRY MUSIC — *A popular style of American music originating in the South and West that usually expresses the feelingful elements of life.*

**SOLO #49
ACCOM. #49-2**

Some Folks Do (SOLO OR DUET)

Whimsically

U.S.

1A / 2A

Some folks like to sigh, Some folks do, Some folks do,

1B / 2B

Some folks like to lie. That's not me or you.

3 ★ Two Birds (4 PART ROUND)

Moderato (M.M. ♩ = 100 -104)

France

1. Once there were two birds sit - ting on a fence; 2. One flew a - way so then there was one.

3. Tra - la, la, la, la, la, la, la, la, la, la; 4. There sat one on - ly one.

4 ★ Rooster Round (5 PART ROUND)

Marcato (M.M. ♩ = 104)

Germany

1. Lis - ten to the Roos - ter make his call. 2. Lis - ten to the Roos - ter make his call.

3. Cock - a - doo - dle - doo, Cock - a - doo, Cock - a - doo. 4. Cock - a - doo - dle - doo, Cock - a -

doo, Cock - a - doo. 5. Cock - a - doo - dle, Cock - a - doo - dle - doo, Cock - a - doo.

? ♫ *Forget the sound of a rhythm pattern? **You Can Look It Up** in the **Rhythm Pattern Dictionary** on pages 46 and 47.*

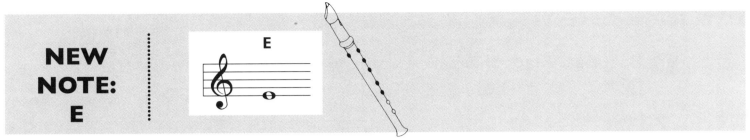

NEW NOTE: E

LISTEN AND PLAY #50

1 Rain, Rain (LISTEN AND PLAY)

Accompaniment Only on Repeat

Expressively

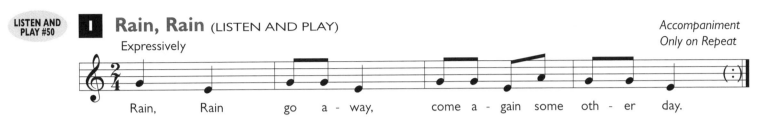

Rain,   Rain   go   a - way,   come a - gain some oth - er   day.

IMPROVISATION — *The art of creating music spontaneously, during performance. Also, a form of composition.*

LISTEN AND IMPROVISE #50

2 ★ SOLO Listen and Improvise Variations on Rain, Rain "By Ear"

Use the tones of the E minor Pentatonic Scale: E - G - A - B - D

TONALITY — *A characteristic of Western music referring to the relationship of pitches to a specific tonal center. If Do is the tonal center, the tonality is Major. If La is the tonal center, the tonality is Minor.*

SOLO #51 ACCOM. #51-2

3 Au Clair de la Lune (IN MINOR TONALITY)

French Folk Song

Legato

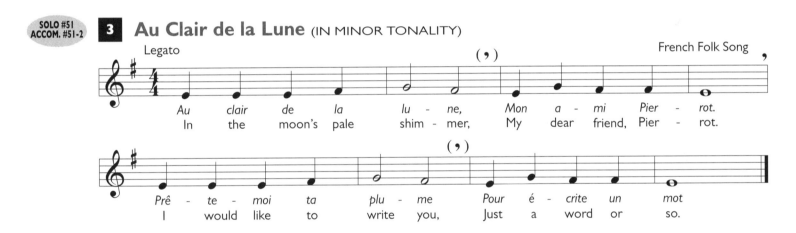

Au   clair   de   la   lu - ne,   Mon   a - mi   Pier - rot.
In   the   moon's   pale   shim - mer,   My   dear   friend, Pier - rot.

Prê - te - moi   ta   plu - me   Pour   é - crite   un   mot
I   would   like   to   write   you,   Just   a   word   or   so.

SOLO #52 ACCOM. #52-2

4 Fais do do (IN MINOR TONALITY)

French Lullaby

Fais   do - do,   Co - las,   mon p'tit   fre - re,   Fais   do - do,   T'au - ras,   du lo - lo.
Go   to   sleep my   sweet lit - tle   bro - ther, Go   to   sleep,   and   you'll get a   treat.

5 S'evivon Round (Spin, My Top)

Not too slowly M.M. ♩ = 132

Hebrew Song

S'e - vi - von,   sov,   sov,   sov,   Ha - nu - kah____ hu   hag   tov,
Spin,   my   top   'round   and   'round,   Ha - nu - kah____ days   we   love,

Ha - nu - kah,   hu   hag   tov,   s'e - vi - von,   sov,   sov,   sov.
Glow - ing   lights,   joy - ful   sounds,   spin,   my   top   'round   and   'round.

20

D.C. AL FINE — *Go back to the beginning and end at the Fine.*

BLUES ROCK — *A musical style that merges blues harmonies with rock and roll rhythms of the 1950s and 1960s.*

SPECIAL PROJECT — **Blues Rock "Call and Response"**

3 ★ **SOLO Blues Rock** (IMITATED "CALL AND RESPONSE")

Each pattern will start on G.
Use the tones G, E, and A.

4 ★★ **SOLO Blues Rock** (IMPROVISED "CALL AND RESPONSE")

Use the tones E, G, A, B♭, and C.

OPTIONAL NEW NOTE:
B♭

5 **The Birch Tree** (THEME FROM THE FOURTH SYMPHONY)

Andante

Russian Folk Song
Tschaikovsky (1840-1893)

? *Forget the meaning of something?* **You Can Look It Up** *in the* **Music Terms Dictionary** *on pages 42, 43, 44, and 45.*

SOLO #56
ACCOM. #56-2

1 ## By the Fireside (SOLO, DUET, TRIO, OR QUARTET)

Lightly

U.S.

1.2. Praise the friend - ly 1. camp fire   Praise its warmth and beau - ty;
2. glow of fire.

Fire, Fire Burn - ing bright, Crack - ling flames light up the night.

2 ## Accompaniment One to By the Fireside

Softly

3 ## Accompaniment Two to By the Fireside

Softly and lightly

4 ## ★ Obbligato to By the Fireside

Softly and lightly

1ST AND 2ND ENDINGS —

1. 2.

Play from the beginning to the repeat sign in the first ending. Then, return to the beginning. On the repeat, skip the first ending and continue through the second ending.

SOLO #57
ACCOM. #57-2

5 ## Nonsense Song

Marcato

Hungary

1. 2.

I just caught a mos - qui - to big - ger than a horse, Oh! house, Oh! If you think so
Rode it up and all a - round high - er than a

you are dim, dim - mer than a horse, Oh! If you think so you are dim, dim - mer than a horse, Oh!

OPTIONAL NEW NOTE:

E

Half hole

SOLO #58
ACCOM. #58-2

6 ## Hatikvah

With expression

Hebrew Melody

NEW NOTE: D

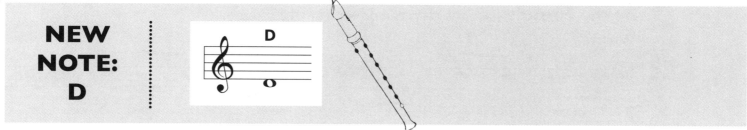

D.C. AL FINE — *Go back to the beginning and end at the Fine.*

SOLO #59
ACCOM. #60

1 Twinkle, Twinkle, Little Star (SOLO, DUET, TRIO, OR QUARTET)

Smoothly

French Folk Tune
Text by Jane and Ann Taylor (1806)

Twin - kle, Twin - kle, lit - tle star, How I won - der what you are.

Up a - bove the world so high, Like a dia - mond in the sky.

2 Harmony Part One to Twinkle, Twinkle, Little Star

Softly and smoothly

3 Harmony Part Two to Twinkle, Twinkle, Little Star

Softly and smoothly

4 ★ Obbligato to Twinkle, Twinkle, Little Star

Softly and smoothly

SWING STYLE — *A type of Big Band jazz of the late 1930s and 1940s.*

SOLO #61
ACCOM. #62

5 ★★ SOLO Twinkle, Twinkle, Little Star (SWING STYLE "BY EAR" STARTING ON D)

SOLO #56
ACCOM. #56-2

1 By the Fireside (SOLO, DUET, TRIO, OR QUARTET)

Lightly
U.S.

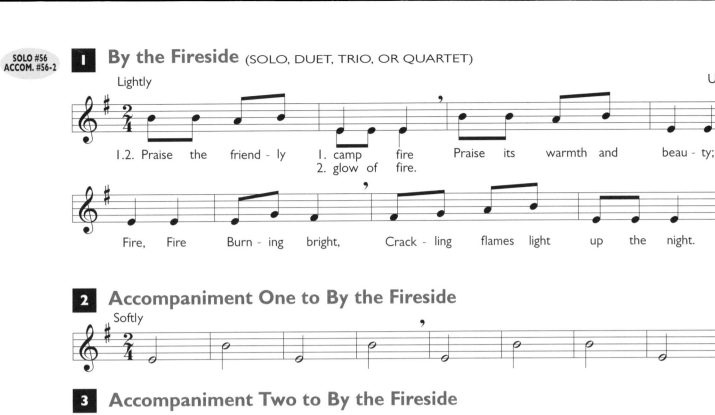

1.2. Praise the friend - ly 1. camp fire Praise its warmth and beau - ty;
2. glow of fire.

Fire, Fire Burn - ing bright, Crack - ling flames light up the night.

2 Accompaniment One to By the Fireside

Softly

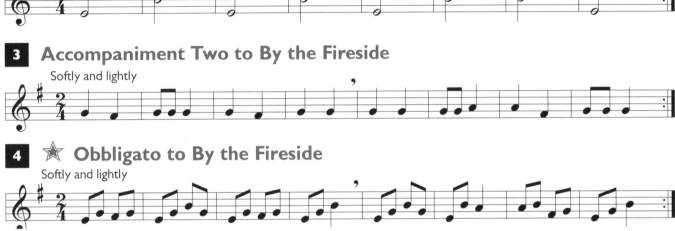

3 Accompaniment Two to By the Fireside

Softly and lightly

4 ★ Obbligato to By the Fireside

Softly and lightly

IST AND 2ND ENDINGS —

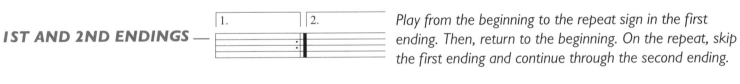

Play from the beginning to the repeat sign in the first ending. Then, return to the beginning. On the repeat, skip the first ending and continue through the second ending.

SOLO #57
ACCOM. #57-2

5 Nonsense Song

Marcato
Hungary

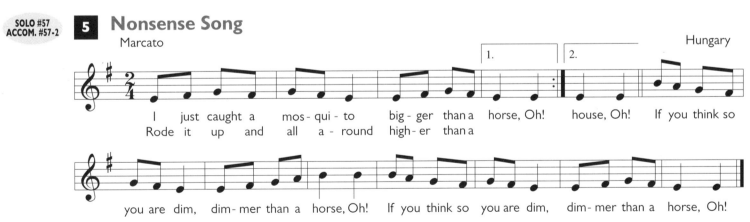

1. 2.

I just caught a mos - qui - to big - ger than a horse, Oh! house, Oh! If you think so
Rode it up and all a - round high - er than a

you are dim, dim - mer than a horse, Oh! If you think so you are dim, dim - mer than a horse, Oh!

OPTIONAL NEW NOTE:
E
Half hole

SOLO #58
ACCOM. #58-2

6 Hatikvah

With expression
Hebrew Melody

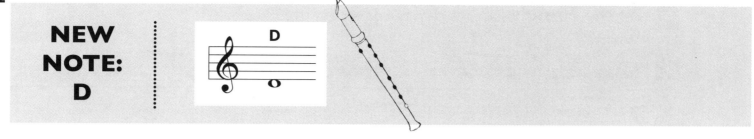

NEW NOTE: D

D.C. AL FINE — *Go back to the beginning and end at the Fine.*

SOLO #59
ACCOM. #60

1 Twinkle, Twinkle, Little Star (SOLO, DUET, TRIO, OR QUARTET)

French Folk Tune
Text by Jane and Ann Taylor (1806)

Twin - kle, Twin - kle, lit - tle star, How I won - der what you are.

Up a - bove the world so high, Like a dia - mond in the sky.

2 Harmony Part One to Twinkle, Twinkle, Little Star

Softly and smoothly

3 Harmony Part Two to Twinkle, Twinkle, Little Star

Softly and smoothly

4 ★ Obbligato to Twinkle, Twinkle, Little Star

Softly and smoothly

SWING STYLE — *A type of Big Band jazz of the late 1930s and 1940s.*

SOLO #61
ACCOM. #62

5 ★★ SOLO Twinkle, Twinkle, Little Star (SWING STYLE "BY EAR" STARTING ON D)

AURAL TRANSPOSITION — *The process of playing a song or passage on a different starting note "by ear" without the aid of music notation.*

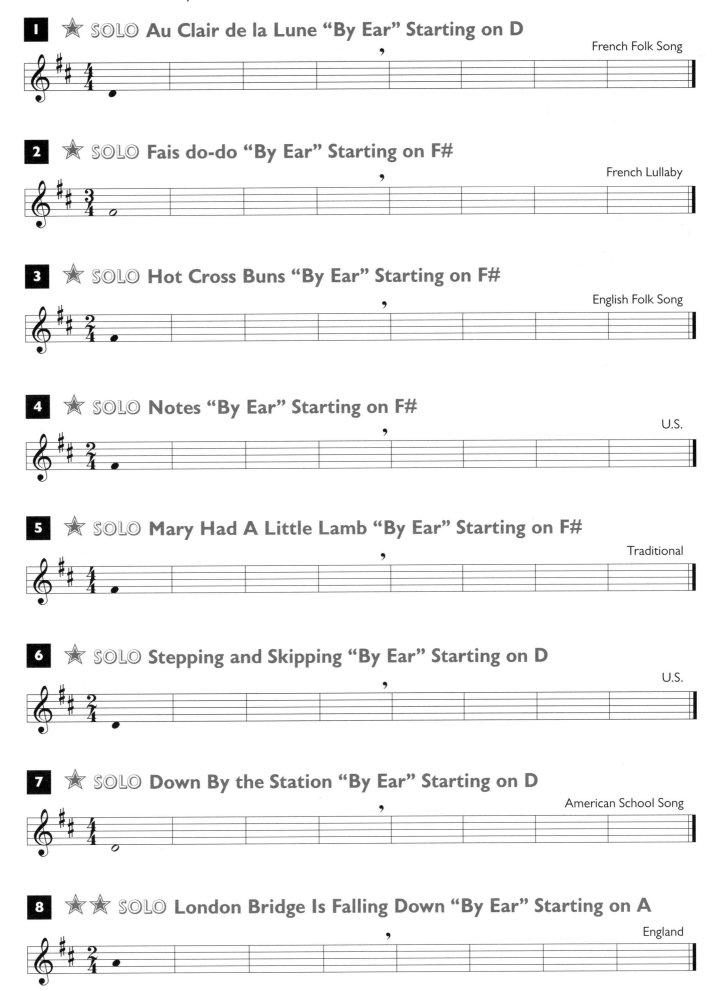

1 ★ SOLO **Au Clair de la Lune "By Ear" Starting on D**

French Folk Song

2 ★ SOLO **Fais do-do "By Ear" Starting on F#**

French Lullaby

3 ★ SOLO **Hot Cross Buns "By Ear" Starting on F#**

English Folk Song

4 ★ SOLO **Notes "By Ear" Starting on F#**

U.S.

5 ★ SOLO **Mary Had A Little Lamb "By Ear" Starting on F#**

Traditional

6 ★ SOLO **Stepping and Skipping "By Ear" Starting on D**

U.S.

7 ★ SOLO **Down By the Station "By Ear" Starting on D**

American School Song

8 ★★ SOLO **London Bridge Is Falling Down "By Ear" Starting on A**

England

SOLO #43
ACCOM. #43-2

1 **Little Tom Tinker** (4 PART ROUND)
Lively

Traditional Round

Lit - tle Tom Tin - ker got burned by a clink - er and he be - gan to cry.

"Ma!"_____ "Ma!"_____ Poor lit - tle in - no - cent guy.

ACCOM. #43-2

2 **Variation on Little Tom Tinker**

Tom - my Tin - ker cried and cried. "Ma!"___ "Ma!"___ my, oh, my.

SOLO #44
ACCOM. #44-2

3 **Oats, Peas, Beans**
Lively

England

Oats, peas, beans and bar - ley grow, Oats, peas, beans and bar - ley grow; Can

you or I or an - y - one know how Oats, peas, beans and bar - ley grow?

4 **Early Round**
Brightly (♩. = 112)

Traditional

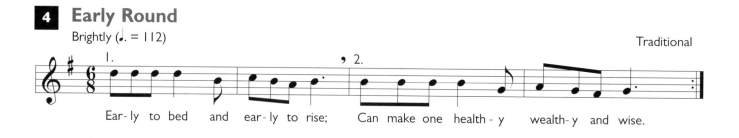

Ear - ly to bed and ear - ly to rise; Can make one health - y wealth - y and wise.

5 **Challenge Round 1**
Lightly (♩. = 100-104)

U.S.

6 **Challenge Round 2**

U.S.

Challenge Rounds 1 and 2 may be played simultaneously.

1 Little Bells of Westminster (4 PART ROUND)
Lightly (M.M. ♩ = 108)

Lit - tle bells of West - min - ster go Ding, Dong, Ding, Dong, Dong,

2 Variation One of Little Bells of Westminster

Lit - tle bells go Ding, Dong, Ding, Dong,

3 Variation Two of Little Bells of Westminster

Bells go Ding, Dong.

The Bells of Westminster, Variation One, and Variation Two may be played simultaneously.

CANON — *Literally, a "rule" for realizing a composition. The rule dictates that each voice imitates exactly the melody sung or played by the first voice.*

PICK-UP — *One or more notes that come before the first full measure of a piece. They are usually found in the last measure.*

4 Tallis Canon (4 VOICE CANON)
Legato* (M.M. ♩ = 96)   Thomas Tallis (1510-1585)

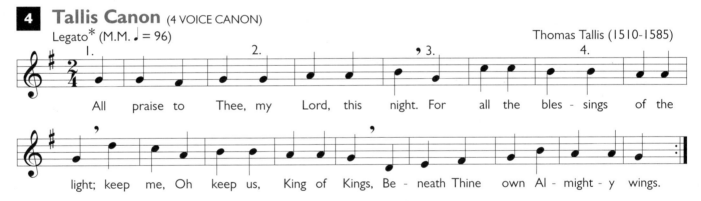

All praise to Thee, my Lord, this night. For all the bles - sings of the

light; keep me, Oh keep us, King of Kings, Be - neath Thine own Al - might - y wings.

5 Doctor Fell (4 PART ROUND)
Marcato* (M.M. ♩ = 100)   Dutch Round

1. I do not like thee, Doc - tor Fell, The rea - son why I can - not tell;
2. But this I know, and know full well, I do not like thee, Doc - tor Fell.

SOLO #63
ACCOM. #63-2

6 Patsy Ory-Ory-Aye
Lively   Irish Railroad Song

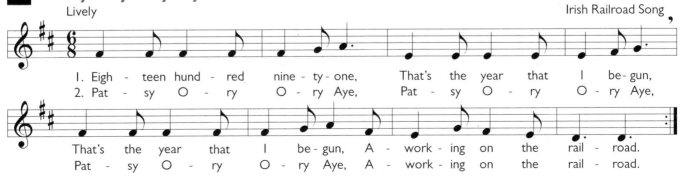

1. Eigh - teen hund - red nine - ty-one, That's the year that I be - gun,
2. Pat - sy O - ry O - ry Aye, Pat - sy O - ry O - ry Aye,

That's the year that I be - gun, A - work - ing on the rail - road.
Pat - sy O - ry O - ry Aye, A - work - ing on the rail - road.

? *Forget the meaning of something?* **You Can Look It Up** *in the* **Music Terms Dictionary** *on pages 42, 43, 44, and 45.*

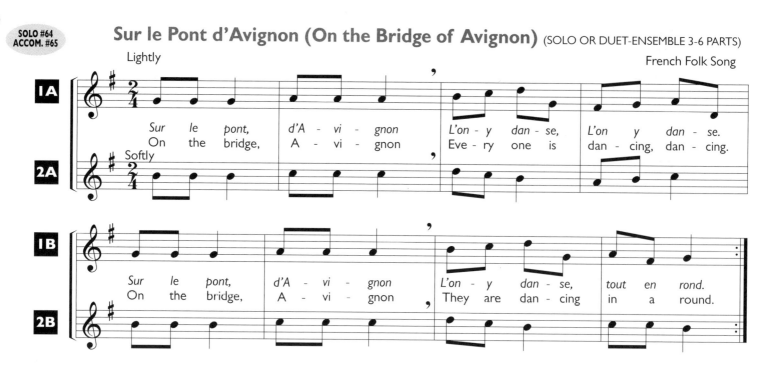

Sur le Pont d'Avignon (On the Bridge of Avignon) (SOLO OR DUET-ENSEMBLE 3-6 PARTS)

SOLO #64
ACCOM. #65

French Folk Song

OSTINATO — *A melodic pattern that is repeated over and over to accompany a principal melody.*

Melodic Ostinatos to Sur le Pont d'Avignon

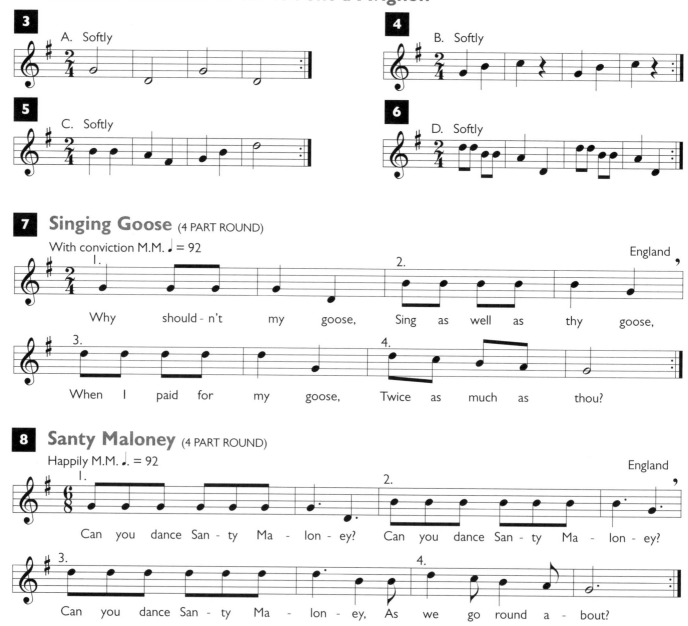

? ♫ *Forget the sound of a rhythm pattern?* **You Can Look It Up** *in the* **Rhythm Pattern Dictionary** *on pages 46 and 47.*

LATIN ROCK — *A musical style mixing characteristics of Rock and Roll with African and Latin American rhythms.*

SOLO #66
ACCOM. #67

1 **Juba** (SOLO, DUET, OR TRIO)

Playfully

African-American Play Song

Ju - ba this and Ju - ba that. Ju - ba chased a yel - low cat.

Ju - ba up and Ju - ba down. Ju - ba run - ning all a - round.

2 **Harmony Part to Juba**

3 ★ **Obbligato to Juba**

ACCOM. #67

4 ★★★ SOLO **Improvise melodic variations on Juba**

BOUFFONS — *Costumed dancers of the 15th and 16th centuries.*

SOLO #68
ACCOM. #69

Bouffons (SOLO OR DUET)

Briskly

Thoinot Arbeau (ca. 1519-1595)

28

BRANLE — *A popular French group dance of the 16th century.*

SOLO #70
ACCOM. #70-2 **1** **Merry Branle**

Merrily

Thoinot Arbeau (ca. 1519 - 1595)

SOLO #71
ACCOM. #72 **2** **Jolly Old Saint Nicholas**

Lightly

Anonymous Carol

Jol - ly Old Saint Nich-o-las, lean your ear this way! Don't you tell a

sing - le soul, what I'm going to say; Christ-mas Eve is com - ing soon,

Now my dear old man, whis-per what you'll bring to me. Tell me if you can.

JAZZ BALLAD STYLE — *A slow, expressive vocal style characterized by extended jazz harmonies.*

SOLO #73
ACCOM. #74 **3** ★ SOLO **Jolly Old Saint Nicholas** (JAZZ BALLAD STYLE - "BY EAR" STARTING ON B)

4 **My Dame's Lame, Tame Crane** (4 PART ROUND)

With emotion M.M. ♩ = 100

Old English Round

My dame hath a lame, tame crane, My dame hath a crane that is lame. Do

Pray, gen - tle Jane let my dame's lame, tame crane heal and come home a - gain

? *Forget the fingering of a note?* **You Can Look It Up** *on the* **Fingering Chart** *located on the inside front cover.*

SPIRITUAL — *A religious folk song of the United States. Mainly, of African-American origin, beginning in the 19th century and continuing into the 20th.*

SOLO #75 ACCOM. #76

1 Jacob Drink (SOLO, ENSEMBLE 2-5 PARTS)

U.S. Spiritual Melody

2 Accompaniment Number One to Jacob Drink

3 Accompaniment Number Two to Jacob Drink

4 ★ Obbligato Number One to Jacob Drink

5 ★★ Obbligato Number Two to Jacob Drink

ACCENT — > *A marking to indicate special stress or emphasis upon a certain note.*

STACCATO — *A marking to indicate a detached, separated style of articulation.*

6 The Frogs (4 PART ROUND)

Hear the live-ly song of the frogs in yon-der pond, Crick! Crick! Crick-i-ty Crick! Br–r–r- rump!

7 Variation on The Frogs

Hear the frogs in yon-der pond, Crick! Crick! Crick! Crick! Br–r–r - rump!

SOLO #77
ACCOM. #77-2

1 ## Die Abendglocke (Evening Bells)
Oh, How Lovely Is the Evening (3 PART ROUND)

Smooth and connected

German Round

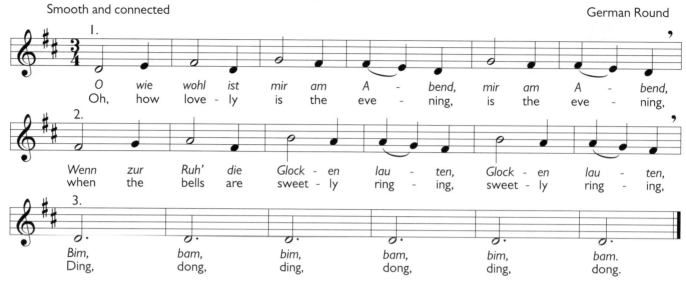

1.
O wie wohl ist mir am A - bend, mir am A - bend,
Oh, how love - ly is the eve - ning, is the eve - ning,

2.
Wenn zur Ruh' die Glock - en lau - ten, Glock - en lau - ten,
when the bells are sweet - ly ring - ing, sweet - ly ring - ing,

3.
Bim, bam, bim, bam, bim, bam.
Ding, dong, ding, dong, ding, dong.

SOLO #78
ACCOM. #78-2

2 ## Cuckoo Song

Swing and Sway

Germany

Cuck - oo, Cuck - oo, wel - come your song; Win - ter is go - ing.

Soft breez - es blow - ing; Spring - time, spring - time soon will be here.

JAZZ WALTZ — *An adaptation of jazz harmonies to 3/4 time characterized by a hard driving bass line and swinging drums, especially in the ride cymbal.*

SOLO #79
ACCOM. #80

3 ★ SOLO **Cuckoo Song** (JAZZ WALTZ STYLE "BY EAR" STARTING ON A)

4 ## Round Evening

Smoothly M.M. ♩. = 56

U.S.

1.   2.   3.   4.

5 ## Round Evening Two

Smoothly M.M. ♩. = 56

U.S.

1.   2.   3.   4.

Round Evening and Round Evening Two may be played simultaneously.

ACCOM. #43-2

1 Row, Row, Row Your Boat (4 PART ROUND)

U.S.
E.O. Lyte

Merrily M.M. ♩. = 92-96

Row, row, row your boat gent - ly down the stream.

Mer - ri - ly mer - ri - ly mer - ri - ly mer - ri - ly Life is but a dream.

2 Variation on Row, Row, Row Your Boat

* *Row, Row, Row Your Boat is a partner tune to Little Tom Tinker (page 24, #1)*

ROCK AND ROLL — *A mid-1950s style of popular music featuring guitar and driving rhythms with accents on the off-beats:* 1 **2** | 1 **2**

SOLO #81
ACCOM. #82

3 Up On the Housetop

Benjamin R. Hanby (U.S. 1833-1867)

Rocking and rolling

Up on the house - top the rein - deer pause, Out jumps good old San - ta Claus;

Down through the chim - ney with lots of toys, All for the lit - tle ones' Christ - mas joys.

Ho, ho, ho, who would - n't go! Ho, ho, ho, who would - n't go!—

Up on the house - top, click, click, click, Down through the chim - ney with good Saint Nick.

SWING STYLE — *"It don't mean a thing if it ain't got that swing."* - Cab Calloway

SOLO #83
ACCOM. #84

4 ☆ SOLO Up On the Housetop (SWING STYLE - "BY EAR" STARTING ON A)

ACCOM. #84

5 ☆☆ SOLO Up On the Housetop (RHYTHMIC IMPROVISATION - SWING STYLE)

? ♫ *Forget the sound of a rhythm pattern?* **You Can Look It Up** *in the* **Rhythm Pattern Dictionary** *on pages 46 and 47.*

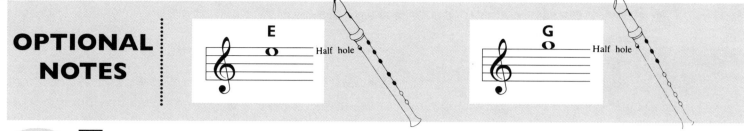

OPTIONAL NOTES

SOLO #85
ACCOM. #85-2

1 Mexican Hat Dance (SOLO, DUET, OR TRIO)

Marcato

Folk Song

2 Harmony Part One to Mexican Hat Dance

3 Harmony Part Two to Mexican Hat Dance

4 Dance A-Round Once

Marcato (M.M. ♩ = 63)

U.S.

5 Dance A-Round Twice

Marcato (M.M. ♩ = 63)

U.S.

6 Dance A-Round Thrice

Marcato (M.M. ♩ = 63)

U.S.

Dance A-Round Once, Twice and Thrice may be played simultaneously.

COUNTRY STYLE — *A popular style of music that originates in the American South and West.*

1 Jingle Bells

Lightly

James Pierpont (U.S. 1822-1893)

Alternate: Jin-gle bells, Jin-gle bells, Jin-gle all the way, Oh! what fun it is to ride

Original: Jin-gle bells, Jin-gle bells, Jin-gle all the way, Oh! what fun it is to ride in a

in an o-pen sleigh.— Jin-gle bells, Jin-gle bells, Jin-gle all the

one horse o-pen sleigh.— Jin-gle bells, Jin-gle bells, Jin-gle all the

way, Oh! what fun it is to ride in an o-pen sleigh.

way, Oh! what fun it is to ride in a one horse o-pen sleigh.

2 Harmony Part One to Jingle Bells

Softly and lightly

3 ★ Harmony Part Two to Jingle Bells

Softly and lightly

SPECIAL PROJECT — Learn to Play a Song "By Ear"

4 ★★★ SOLO Suggestion: Play *We Wish You A Merry Christmas*

Starting on D

5 ★★★ SOLO Suggestion: Play *Oh Hanukkah*

Starting on E

6 ★★★ SOLO Suggestion: Play *Good King Wenceslas*

Starting on G

FOLK HYMN — *A song of worship with a religious text that has been set to a folk melody.*

SOLO #86
ACCOM. #86-2

1 **Amazing Grace**

John Newton (1779)
Early American Melody

Stately

A - maz - ing— grace how sweet the sound that saved a— wretch like— me!—

— I once— was— lost but now I'm— found; Was blind but— now I see.—

GOSPEL — *African-American church music characterized by expression, improvisation, and a strong sense of celebration.*

SOLO #87
ACCOM. #88

2 ★ SOLO **Amazing Grace** (GOSPEL STYLE - "BY EAR" STARTING ON D)

ACCOM. #88

3 ★★ SOLO **Amazing Grace** (IMPROVISE IN GOSPEL STYLE - "BY EAR" STARTING ON D)

SPECIAL PROJECT — **Learn to Play a Song "By Ear"**

4 ★★★ SOLO **Suggestion: Play** *Oh When the Saints Go Marching In*

Starting on G

or D

5 ★★★ SOLO **Suggestion: Play** *On Top of Old Smokey*

Starting on D

BALLAD — *A short, simple song in a narrative or descriptive form,*
sometimes set to a romantic or historical poem.

SOLO #89
ACCOM. #90

6 **Aura Lee**

Gently

American Ballad

As the black-bird in the spring, 'Neath the wil - low tree,

Sat and piped, I heard him sing, Sing - ing Au - ra Lee.

Au - ra Lee, Au - ra Lee, Maid of gold - en hair,

Sun - shine came a - long with thee, And swal - lows in the air.

SOLO #91
ACCOM. #91-2

1 Sleep, Baby, Sleep (Schlaf, Kindlein, Schlaf)

Legato

German Lullaby

Schlaf, Kind-lein, schlaf, Der Va - ter hüt' die Schaf,
Sleep, ba - by, sleep, Thy fa - ther guards the sheep,

Die Mut - ter schüt - telt's
Thy mo - ther shakes the

Bäum - e - lein, Da fällt her - ab ein Träum - e - lein,
dream - land tree, And from it fall sweet dreams for thee,

Schlaf, Kind - lein, schaf.
Sleep, ba - by, sleep.

TENUTO — A term used to indicate a sustained (connected) style of articulation. Horizontal dashes above or below a series of notes also indicate a sustained style of articulation.

2 Harmony Part to Sleep, Baby, Sleep

Tenuto

3 ☆ Obbligato to Sleep, Baby, Sleep

Lightly

4 The Hart, He Loves the High Wood (4 PART ROUND)

With humor and enthusiasm M.M. ♩ = 132

Composer Unknown c. 1680

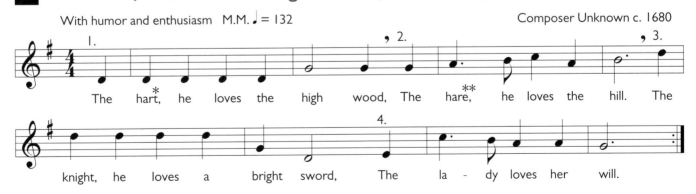

The hart, he loves the high wood, The hare, he loves the hill. The

knight, he loves a bright sword, The la - dy loves her will.

* A hart is an adult male deer.

** A hare is a field animal similar to a rabbit, but larger.

? Forget the sound of a rhythm pattern? **You Can Look It Up** in the **Rhythm Pattern Dictionary** on pages 46 and 47.

36

ACCELERANDO POCO A POCO — *Faster, little by little.*

SOLO #92
ACCOM. #93

1 The Shining Moon

Accelerando poco a poco

Russian Folk Tune

2 Variation One on The Shining Moon

Accelerando poco a poco

SYNCOPATION — *A displacement of the natural pulse or accent of the music, usually to the second half of the beat, as in:*

3 ★ Variation Two on The Shining Moon

Accelerando poco a poco

4 Variation Three on The Shining Moon

Accelerando poco a poco

1 ⭐⭐ **Variation Four on The Shining Moon**

Accelerando poco a poco

2 **Variation Five on The Shining Moon**

Accelerando poco a poco

3 ⭐⭐⭐ **Variation Six on The Shining Moon**

Accelerando poco a poco

4 **Variation Seven on The Shining Moon**

Accelerando poco a poco

? *Forget the meaning of something?* **You Can Look It Up** in the **Music Terms Dictionary** on pages 42, 43, 44, and 45.

38

1 Scotland's Burning (IN TWO- QUARTER TIME)

2 Variation on Scotland's Burning

3 Scotland's A-Burning (IN SIX-EIGHT TIME)

4 Variation on Scotland's A-Burning

5 Sing Noel (3 PART ROUND)

NEW NOTE: F

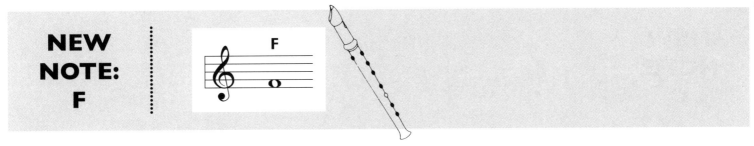

F

SOLO #27
ACCOM. #27-2

Waltz (SOLO OR DUET)
Brightly - in one to the bar

19th Century Dance Tune

3 ## Thou, Poor Bird (4-PART ROUND)
M.M. ♩ = 100-108

Anonymous

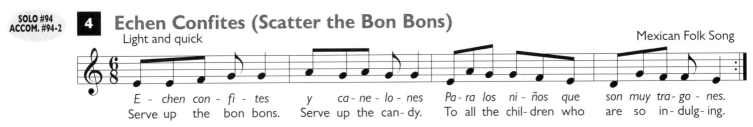

Thou, poor bird, Mourn'st the tree, Where

sweet - ly thou didst war - ble In thy wan - d'rings free.

SOLO #94
ACCOM. #94-2

4 ## Echen Confites (Scatter the Bon Bons)
Light and quick

Mexican Folk Song

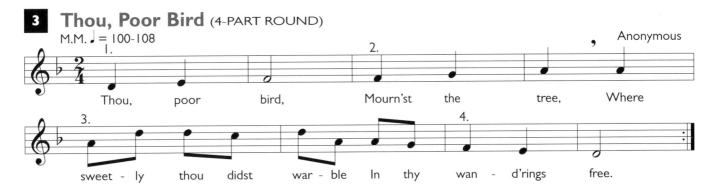

E - chen con - fi - tes y ca - ne - lo - nes Pa - ra los ni - ños que son muy tra - go - nes.
Serve up the bon bons. Serve up the can - dy. To all the chil - dren who are so in - dulg - ing.

SOLO #95
ACCOM. #96

5 ## Intry Mintry
Playfully

Game Song

In - try min - try cu - try corn. Ap - ple seed and ap - ple thorn.
Turn and turn and turn a - bout. O - U - T and that spells OUT!!

ACCOM. #96

6 ⭐ SOLO **Improvise Rhythmic Variations on** *Intry Mintry*

ACCOM. #96

7 ⭐⭐ SOLO **Improvise Melodic Variations on** *Intry Mintry*

Use tones of the D Minor Pentatonic Scale:

D F G A C (D)

ACCOM. #96

8 ⭐⭐⭐ SOLO **Improvise Melodic Variations on** *Intry Mintry*

Use tones of the D Dorian Scale:

D E F G A B C

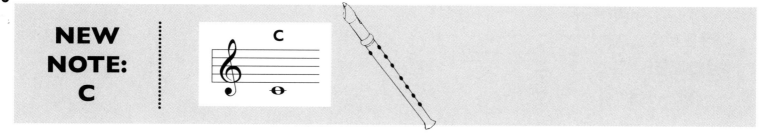

NEW NOTE: C

CONDUCTUS — *A 12th century song with a serious, usually sacred, text in Latin verse.*

SOLO #97
ACCOM. #97-2

1 Song of the Donkey (MIXOLYDIAN MODE)

Smoothly   12th Century Conductus

O - ri - en - tis   par - ti - bus   Ad - ven - ta - vit   a - si - nus   Pul - cher et for

tis - si - mus   Sar - ci - nis ap - tis - si - mus,   Hez,   Sir   As - ne   hez.

2 Tide and Time (2 PART ROUND)

Marcato   M.M. ♩ = 100-108   Lowell Mason (1864)

Time   and   tide   will   wait   for   no - one

SOLO #98
ACCOM. #99

3 Scarborough Fair (DORIAN MODE)

Smoothly with expression   English Ballad

Are   you   going   to   Scar - bo - rough   Fair?_____ Pars - ley,

sage,   rose - mar - y,   and   thyme._____ Oh,

send   my   love   to   one   who   lives   there,_____ Once   she

was   a   true   love   of   mine._____

SPECIAL PROJECTS — DO IT! IMPROVISE

SOLO #20
ACCOM. #21

1 ### Cobbler, Cobbler (PAGE 9)

Rhythmically

Jamaican Street Song

Cob - bler, Cob - bler fix my shoe, Get it done by half past two.

Half past two, I'm at your door, Get it done by half past four.

⭐⭐ **SOLO** Improvise Melodic Variations on *Cobbler, Cobbler*

Use tones of the C Pentatonic Scale:

C D E G A (C) (D)

LISTEN AND
PLAY #50

2 ### Rain, Rain (PAGE 19)

Expressively

*Accompaniment
Only on Repeat*

Rain, Rain go a - way, come a - gain some oth - er day.

⭐⭐⭐ **SOLO** Listen and Improvise Melodic Variations on *Rain, Rain*

Use tones of the E Phrygian Scale:

E F G A B C D E

SOLO #30
ACCOM. #32

3 ### The Blues in D (PAGE 12)

In a swinging style

⭐⭐⭐ **SOLO** Improvise Melodic Variations on *The Blues in D*

Use tones of the D Blues Scale:

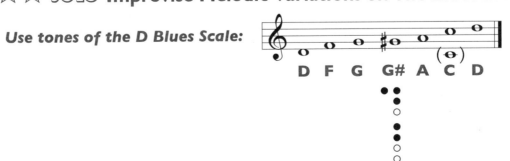

D F G G# A C D

? *Forget the fingering of a note?* **You Can Look It Up** on the **Fingering Chart** located on the inside front cover.

MUSIC TERMS DICTIONARY
DEFINITIONS NEEDED TO UNDERSTAND MUSIC TERMINOLOGY

Accelerando poco a poco	"Faster, little by little."
Animato	In an excited, animated style.
Accent	"Look It Up" in the *Music Signs and Symbols Dictionary* - page 4.
Accidental	A flat, sharp, or natural sign that alters the pitch of a note.
Adagio	See **Tempo Markings** - page 45.
Al fine	To the end.
Allegro	See **Tempo Markings** - page 45.
Andante	See **Tempo Markings** - page 45.
Aural Transposition	A process of playing a song or passage on a different starting note "by ear" without the aid of music notation.
Ballad	A short, simple song in a narrative or descriptive form, sometimes set to a romantic or historical poem.
Bar Line	"Look It Up" in the *Music Signs and Symbols Dictionary* - page 4.
Barcarolle	Originally, a folk song of the Venetian gondoliers (boatmen of the city of Venice).
Blue Grass	A type of Anglo-American folk music originating around the mid-1940s in rural Appalachia.
Blues	An African-American folk music characterized by spontaneity and deep emotion.
Blues Rock	A musical style that merges blues harmonies with rock and roll rhythms of the 1950s and 1960s.
Blues Scale	A six tone scale used to improvise over blues harmonies.
Branle	A popular French group dance of the 16th century in which all motions of the lead couple are imitated.
Bouffons	Costumed dancers of the 15th and 16th centuries.
Call and Response	A musical alteration between two performers or a performer and a group of performers. The musical response to the call may be imitated or improvised.
Canon	Literally, a "rule" for realizing a composition. The rule dictates that each voice imitates exactly the melody sung or played by the first voice.
Clef	"Look It Up" in the *Music Signs and Symbols Dictionary* - page 4.
Conductus	A 12th century song with a serious, usually sacred text in Latin verse.
Country Music	A popular style of American music originating in the South and West that usually expresses the feelingful elements of life.
Country Swing	A blend of western, bluegrass, and swing styles originating in Texas during the 1940s.
D.C. al Fine	An abbreviation for "Da Capo al Fine," which means "go back to the beginning and end at the *Fine.*"
D.S.	An abbreviation for "Dal Signo," which means "go back and repeat from the sign."

Dance Music	Music used to form the context for synchronous and expressive movement.
Dolce	"Sweetly."
Dorian Mode	See **Mode** - page 44.
Double Bar Line	"Look It Up" in the *Music Signs and Symbols Dictionary* - page 4.
Duet	A composition for two performers.
Dynamics	Degrees of softness to loudness.

	ppp/pianississimo	very, very soft
	pp/pianissimo	very soft
	p/piano	soft
	mp/mezzo piano	medium soft
	mf/mezzo forte	medium loud
	f/forte	loud
	ff/fortissimo	very loud
	fff/fortississimo	very, very loud

First and Second Ending	"Look It Up" in the *Music Signs and Symbols Dictionary* - page 4.
Flat	"Look It Up" in the *Music Signs and Symbols Dictionary* - page 4.
Folk Hymn	A song of worship with a religious text that has been set to a folk melody.
Folk Song	A song reflecting the traditions of the people of a country or region and forming part of their characteristic culture.
Gospel	Afro-American church music characterized by expression, improvisation, and a strong sense of celebration.
Harmony	Two or more different tones played or sung at the same time.
Honky Tonk	A rowdy musical style characterized by a lively piano accompaniment.
Hymn	A song of worship.
Improvisation	The art of creating music spontaneously, during performance. Also, a form of composition.
Jazz	Originally, a style of improvised dance music characterized by strong rhythms and expressiveness, originating in the South by Black Americans.
Jazz Ballad	A slow, expressive vocal style characterized by extended jazz harmonies.
Jazz Waltz	An adaptation of jazz harmonies to 3/4 time characterized by a hard driving bass line and swinging drums, especially in the ride cymbal.
Key Signature	"Look It Up" in the *Music Signs and Symbols Dictionary* - page 4.
Latin Rock	A musical style mixing characteristics of rock and roll with African and Latin American rhythms.
Legato	"With a smooth, connected style of articulation."
Lullaby	A cradle song usually sung by a mother to soothe or quiet an infant before bedtime.
Major Tonality	See **Tonality** - page 45.
Marcato	Articulation with marked emphasis on each tone.
Measure	"Look It Up" in the *Music Signs and Symbols Dictionary* - page 4.
Metronome Marking	A precise indication of the speed of the beat as expressed by Maelzel's Metronome. (The Metronome is a machine with a ticking pendulum patented by Johann Maelzel in 1816. M.M. ♩ = 96 means the tempo of the quarter note (crotchet) is 96 beats per minute.)

Minor Tonality	See **Tonality** - page 45.
Mode	A term that embraces many ancient and contemporary concepts regarding the classification of scales and melodies. Today, the term usually refers to seven distinct scales derived from twelve ancient church modes. Below is an example of each mode starting on D.

D Ionian (Major) Mode

do re mi fa so la ti do

D Dorian Mode

re mi fa so la ti do re

D Phrygian Mode

mi fa so la ti do re mi

D Lydian Mode

fa so la ti do re mi fa

D Mixolydian Mode

so la ti do re mi fa so

D Aeolian (Natural Minor) Mode

la ti do re mi fa so la

D Locrian Mode

ti do re mi fa so la ti

Moderato	See **Tempo Markings** - page 45.
Natural	"Look It Up" in the *Music Signs and Symbols Dictionary* - page 4.
Obbligato	An accompanying part, usually ornamental in character.
Ostinato	A melodic pattern repeated over and over to accompany a principal melody.
Pentatonic Scale	A five-tone scale. Examples are notated below:

C Pentatonic — do re mi so la
A Minor Pentatonic — la do re mi so
G Pentatonic — do re mi so la

E Minor Pentatonic — la do re mi so
F Pentatonic — do re mi so la
D Minor Pentatonic — la do re mi so

Pick-up	One or more notes that come before the first full measure of a piece.
Plaintively	"With sadness."
Poco a poco	"Little by little."
Polka	A lively round dance originated by Bohemian (Eastern European) peasants.
Quick Time	A doubling of the tempo that halves the performance time.
Reggae	A musical style mixing African and Caribbean rhythms often attributed to Jamaican sources.
Rest	"Look It Up" in the *Music Signs and Symbols Dictionary* - page 5.
Rhythm	An organizing principle of traditional music comprising three fundamental elements that are heard and felt. 1) A **Primary Beat** - the "basic" or "big" beat usually felt as the marching, walking, or dancing beat. It is also the beat represented by the baton of a conductor. 2) **Meter** - the subdivision of the Primary Beat into twos and threes. **Duple Meter** is the result when the Primary Beat is subdivided into two equal parts. **Triple Meter** is the result when the Primary Beat is subdivided into three equal parts. 3) **Melodic Rhythm** - the rhythm of the melody or the rhythm of the text. It is the result of virtually limitless combinations of beats, subdivisions, and elongations of the beat.

Rock and Roll A mid-1950s style of popular music featuring guitar and driving rhythms with accents on the off-beats: 1 2 3 4 .

Round A specially composed melody that allows two or more individuals to create interesting musical effects by starting the melody at different times.

Scale Literally, a "ladder" or succession of eight tones ascending to or descending from a specified tonic (tonal center) to the tonic (tonal center) above or below. Examples:

D Major Scale

do re mi fa so la ti do

D Harmonic Minor Scale - Ascending

la ti do re mi fa si la

D Melodic Minor Scale - Ascending

la ti do re mi fi si la

D Melodic Minor Scale - Descending

la so fa mi re do ti la

Slur "Look It Up" in the *Music Signs and Symbols Dictionary* - page 5.

Solo One player alone, with or without accompaniment.

Spiritual A religious folk song of African-American origin.

Staccato "Look It Up" in the *Music Signs and Symbols Dictionary* - page 4.

Swing Style A type of Big Band jazz of the late 1930s and 1940s.

Syncopation A displacement of the natural pulse of the music, usually to the second half of the beat as in:

Tempo Rate of speed of the beat.

Tempo Markings

1. Symbols indicating rate of speed.

adagio	slow
andante	moderately slow
moderato	moderate
allegro	lively, brisk
vivace	fast
presto	very fast

2. Symbols indicating change of speed.

accelerando	increase speed
piu mosso	more motion
ritardando	decrease speed
meno mosso	less motion
a tempo	return to previous tempo
rubato	freely, with expression

Tenuto "Look It Up" in the *Music Signs and Symbols Dictionary* - page 4.

Theme and Variations A musical form based upon a melody followed by a succession of composed rhythmic/melodic variations.

Tie "Look It Up" in the *Music Signs and Symbols Dictionary* - page 5.

Time Signature "Look Up" **Measure Signature** in the *Music Signs and Symbols Dictionary* - page 5.

Tonality A characteristic of Western music referring to the relationship of pitches to a specific tonal center. If Do is the tonal center, the tonality is Major. If La is the tonal center, the tonality is is minor.

Treble Clef (G Clef) "Look It Up" in the *Music Signs and Symbols Dictionary* - page 4.

Triplet Three notes of equal value grouped together with a "3" over them.

Waltz A 19th century dance in triple meter.

RHYTHMIC PATTERN DICTIONARY

Hot Cross Buns (p 6 - CD # 1)
Twinkle, Twinkle, Little Star (p 22 - CD # 59)

Waltz (p 11 - CD # 27)
Mexican Hat Dance (p 32 - CD # 85)

Mary Had a Little Lamb (p 6 - CD # 9)
Au Claire de la Lune (p 7 - CD # 12)
Vesper Hymn (p 16 - CD # 46)
Aura Lee (p 34 - CD # 89)

Lightly Row (p 14 - CD # 34)
A Paris (p 16 - CD # 45)

Hot Cross Buns (p 6 - CD # 1)
Shepherd's Hey (p 15 - CD # 38)

Down By the Station (p.7 - CD # 13)
The Birch Tree (p 20 - CD # 55)

Au Claire de la Lune (p 7 - CD # 12)
Down By the Station (p 7 - CD # 13)

Au Claire de la Lune (p 7 - CD # 12)
Aura Lee (p 34 - CD # 89)

Bubble Gum Duet (p 17 - CD # 48)
The Shining Moon (p 36 - CD # 92)

Bubble Gum Duet (p 17 - CD # 48)
Stepping, Skipping and Resting (P. 7 - Variation 3)

Bubble Gum Duet (p 17 - CD # 48)
Shave and a Haircut (p 10)

Taking Turns Duet (p 8)
Bubble Gum Duet (p 17 - CD # 48)

Bubble Gum Duet (p 17 - CD # 48)
The Birch Tree (p 20 - CD # 55)

Hot Cross Buns (p 8 - CD # 5)
Juba (p 9 - CD # 22)
Jolly Old St. Nicholas (p 28 - CD # 71)

Jolly Old St. Nicholas (p 28 - CD # 71)
Baa, Baa, Black Sheep in Minor Tonality (p 20 - CD # 53)
Silent, Silent (p 17 - CD # 47)

The Shining Moon (p 36, 37 - CD # 92)

Jingle Bells (p 33 - CD # 41) **Lightly Row** (p 14 - CD # 34)
On The Bridge of Avignon (p 26 - CD # 64)

Up On the Housetop (p 31 - CD # 81)
Sleep, Baby Sleep (p 35 - CD # 91)

♩ ♫ | ♫ ♩ **Up On the Housetop** (p 31 - CD # 81)

♫ ♩ 𝄽 **Bubble Gum Duet** (p 17 - CD # 48)

𝄽 ♫ **Bubble Gum Duet** (p 17 - CD # 48)

♩. ♪ **The Shining Moon** (p 36 - CD # 92)
Aura Lee (p 34 meas 9 - CD # 89)
Sleep, Baby Sleep (p 35 meas 2 - CD # 91)

♪ ♩ ♪ **The Shining Moon** (p 36 - CD # 92)

𝄾 ♩ ♪ **The Shining Moon** ((p 36 - Variation Two, CD #92)

♩ ♩ ♩ | ♩ ♩ ♩ **Waltz** (p 11 - CD # 27)
Mexican Hat Dance (p 32 - CD # 85)

♩. | ♩. **Oh, How Lovely is the Evening** (p 30- CD # 77)

♩. __ | ♩. **Barcarolle** (p 10 - CD # 24)

𝅗𝅥 𝅗𝅥 **Fais Do Do** (p 7 - CD # 16)
Barcarolle (p 10 - CD # 24)
Scarborough Fair (p 40 - CD # 98)

𝅗𝅥 𝄽 **Waltz Variation 1** (p 11)

♩ ♩ 𝄽 **Waltz Variation 2** (p 11)

♩ 𝄽 𝄽 **Mexican Hat Dance** (p 32 - CD # 85)

♩ 𝄽 ♩ **Mexican Hat Dance** (p 32 - CD # 85)
Waltz Variation 2 (p 11)

𝅗𝅥 ♫ **Amazing Grace** (p 34 - CD # 86)

♩. ♩. **Little Tom Tinker** (p 24 meas 5-6 - CD # 43)
Row, Row, Row Your Boat (p 31)
Patsy Ory-Ory-Aye (p 25 - CD # 63)

♫ ♫ ♫ **Little Tom Tinker** (p 24 - CD # 43)
Echen Confites (p 39 meas 3- CD # 94)

♫ ♫ ♩. **Early Round** (p 16)

♩ ♪ ♩ ♪ **Little Tom Tinker** (p 24 - CD # 43)
Oats, Peas, Beans (p 24 - CD # 44)
Patsy Ory-Ory-Aye (p 25 - CD # 63)

♩ ♪ ♩. **Oats, Peas, Beans** (p 24 - CD # 44)
Patsy Ory-Ory-Aye (p 25 - CD # 63)
Merry Branle (p. 28 - CD - # 70)

♫ ♩ ♪ **Oats, Peas, Beans** (p 24 - CD # 44)
Merry Branle (p. 28 - CD - # 70)

♫ ♪ ♩ **Echen Confites** (p 39 meas 3- CD # 94)

CD MUSIC INDEX